Distributed by
Nataraj Books
P.O. Box 5076
Springfield, VA 22150

WOLFGANG ZIEGLER · NEPAL

Wolfgang Ziegler

NEPAL

Himalayan Books
New Delhi

The author and the publisher thanks
Dr. Gottfried-Berger for the photographs on
pages 63 and 64 and on the back cover.
All other pictures have been provided by the
author.

First Published, 1988 by
Himalayan Books, New Delhi-110013

Printed and Bound in Singapore
in collaboration with Toppan & Co (S) Pte.

Distributed by
The English Book Store
17-L, Connaught Place
New Delhi-110001 (India)

Photographs © Wolfhart Verlag, Vienna, 1988

English Text © Himalayan Books, 1988

ISBN 81 7002 024 7

Namaste: I greet the Divine in You

Nepal, the mysterious kingdom in the Himalayas, was one of those unexplored regions of the earth, which resisted the advances of the Europeans for a long span of time. Long after Columbus and Magellan had undertaken their expeditions, and Jesuits had been engaged in missionary activities in far-off Peking and in Tibet, stories about a kingdom locked amidst mountains started reaching attentive ears in the west. This information came from missionaries, who had succeeded in crossing the Himalayas from the northern side. Around A.D. 1661/1662, two Jesuits, namely, Albert d'Orville and Johann Gruber, who hailed, respectively, from Belgium and Linz, reached the Kathmandu Valley of the city-kingdoms. To these travellers, this strange, exotic country must have appeared fascinating as well as awe-inspiring. Through these initial contacts the relations between Nepal and Europe altered only to the extent that the country figured in geographical works. The situation changed only in the eighteenth century A.D. when under the leadership of the Shah dynasty the Gurkhas conquered the Valley from the western side and pressed for further expansion. British troops withstood the threat from the north, and a Peace Treaty was obtained from Nepal by force. In accordance with the treaty, a British Resident was stationed in Kathmandu, and the country came under the surveillance of the British. Thus peace was ensured on the northern frontier of the sub-continent.

The Rana rulers of the nineteenth century carried on a reign of excessive exploitation, to which the huge palaces in the vicinity of Kathmandu bear ample witness. Since the bloodless revolution in the beginning of the fifties of this century, Nepal has been a country with a constitution subservient to the King, who, though an absolute monarch, does not rule autocratically. The highest authority of the State and of the judiciary is vested in him, though, as everywhere else, the support of the aristocracy and the clergy has always been essential for a ruler. For his subjects, King Birendra is a divine manifestation, an incarnation of god Vishnu. Though Hinduism is the state religion in Nepal, there exists complete freedom as to the practice of religion. Tibetan Buddhism has latterly come into prominence due to the influx of Tibetan refugees. In the Kathmandu Valley the religions of the Indo-Aryan Hindus of the south are mixed with those of the Tibeto-Buddhist people of the north, resulting in a unique blend. These religions have influenced one another appreciably. Despite a tolerant attitude towards other religions, missionary activities have not been permitted in the Kingdom since the eighteenth century, and, as a result, the Christian Orders have restricted themselves to humanitarian work.

The conventional greeting 'Namaste' itself is symbolic of the strong bonds between man and his religion.

The Country under the Roof of the World

Nepal separates the giants, India and China, in the form of a broad wedge. It has a surface area of 144,000 sq.km. and is situated at the same latitude as North Egypt. The country has the steepest slopes in the world. The Himalayan giants towering more than 8000 metres don't form any watersheds despite their huge proportions. Amidst the foothills, which have an average height of 3000 metres, the Kathmandu Valley, with its city kingdoms, lies at a height of about 1300 metres. In the south, the tropical forest area of the Terai slopes towards the Indian plains. The high altitude and the proximity of mountains ensure a mild climate.

Nepal has approximately 13 million inhabitants. A very small percentage of this population lives in the Kathmandu Valley. The official language is Nepali, which is derived from Gurkhali and has been enriched by numerous words from regional dialects. The Newars of the Kathmandu Valley have their own language, Newari, which has a considerable literary tradition. The Sherpas, who live in northern Nepal, speak a modified form of Tibetan.

More than 90 per cent of the population lives on agriculture. Tourism and industry have been progressing, but these hopeful developments can pose some problems as well to the country. Extensive land reforms are intended to help the farmers, so that they do not fall preys to the caprices of the landlords. The caste system, though officially abolished in 1963, has not really lost its hold. In the eyes of the law, however, all citizens have equal rights.

The major problems of the country, such as the population explosion, high infant mortality, shortcomings in the educational policy and inadequate medical facilities, are quite evident to the intelligent tourist. And, he or she notices that a high percentage of the population is under-nourished and suffers from lung diseases. Malaria and typhoid are widespread. Life-expectancy is below fifty years. Though many new schools have been opened, illiteracy is around 80 per cent. Environmental problems have surfaced of late. Deforestation has taken place to such an extent that barely 25 per cent of the surface area is now covered with forests. Consequently, soil erosion continues apace. The population explosion postulates full exploitation of the available cultivable land. The terrace-type cultivation, which has been in vogue since ages, is being continuously extended to bigger units of land. People have been working towards the solutions of many of these problems. In a country, which has few good roads and rail connections, and which is handicapped by a number of infrastructural shortcomings, it will, of necessity, take time to bring about the much-needed improvements. These will depend not only on the developmental efforts of the Nepalese themselves, but also on the help which the western industrial nations may be ready to provide.

Kathmandu; Indra Chowk:
Statue of the 'sentinel' guarding
the temple of Akasha Bhairava.

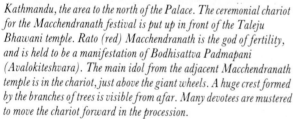

Kathmandu, the area to the north of the Palace. The ceremonial chariot for the Macchendranath festival is put up in front of the Taleju Bhawani temple. Rato (red) Macchendranath is the god of fertility, and is held to be a manifestation of Bodhisattva Padmapani (Avalokiteshvara). The main idol from the adjacent Macchendranath temple is in the chariot, just above the giant wheels. A huge crest formed by the branches of trees is visible from afar. Many devotees are mustered to move the chariot forward in the procession.

Nobody feels disturbed when children climb on the guardian figures in front of the Taleju Bhawani temple. The Kailasha vase on the wall is a Tantric symbol of luck and points to the origin of goddess Taleju Bhawani.

The awe-inspiring figure of Kala Bhairava occupies the centre of the Durbar Square in Kathmandu.

Lord Shiva in his destructive form; the figure has been cut from a single rock in the form of a relief. The six-armed statue is painted in loud colours and wears a tiara of skulls. Snakes are wreathed round the deity's neck. A big garland of human skulls is symbolic of the ferocity of Kala Bhairava. He stands on the demon, Vetala, the embodiment of ignorance. In popular belief, Kala Bhairava helps devotees to probe the truth, for anyone telling a lie before him is said to bleed to death at once. (right)

Children climb on the rat, the mount of Ganesha, to whom the small temple behind the Kastamandapa (in Kathmandu) is dedicated. The shrine, Ashoka Vinayakar, is one of the four important temples dedicated to Ganesha.

Kathmandu: The Taleju Bhawani temple, towering in the north of the Palace complex, surpasses all the temples in Nepal in its size and grandeur. King Mahendra (1560–1574 A.D.) is said to have been entrusted by the goddess herself, with the job of constructing the first three-storeyed temple in Nepal. Its immensity is enhanced considerably by the big, steep substructure. When her new abode was ready, the Tantric goddess entered it in the form of a bee. The ground plan of the building exhibits a Mandala. *The white structure in the foreground is part of the King's palace.*

Kings from Time Immemorial

A Buddhist legend of creation says that in hoary times the entire Kathmandu Valley was a huge lake. As a matter of fact, during the last phase of the formation of mountains through land-elevation and damming, huge mountain lakes were formed: these silted up around 200,000 years ago. The Chinese Bodhisattva, Manjushri, made a pilgrimage to the godhead, Swayambhu (the Adi Buddha), who, in the form of a flame, swam on these waters on a lotus. The holy man decided that the Valley should be brought under cultivation. With the thrust of his sword in the solid ground, he carved the gorge of Chvor. Thus, he created the only outflow from the Kathmandu Valley which exists today. Manjushri founded a colony, installed a king on the throne and then returned to China.

Not much research has been done on the early history of Nepal. There are hardly any written records thereof. Only a few names from the early ruling dynasties, whose authenticity is open to doubt, have come down to us. The twenty-nine kings of the first great dynasty, the Kiratis, ruled Nepal for more than a thousand years. The historical Buddha is said to have lived during the reign of the seventh Kirati King. The legend of a journal, recorded by the (north) Indian emperor Ashoka (263–233 B.C.), on his journey, has not been substantiated. Important specimens of workmanship in stone—masonry dating from the times of the Licchavis (467–740 A.D.)—have, however, been preserved. The oldest inscription in Nepal, which is on a stone column, describes the first Licchavi king, Manendra, during whose reign trade with Tibet and China, and the development of an irrigation system, are said to have begun.

The urban culture of the Licchavis was destroyed in the 8th century A.D. and was superseded by the Thakurs who retained power till the 13th century. The Kathmandu Valley then came under the Malla dynasty. This ruling family had

The Palace in Kathmandu:
Window facing Nasal Chowk in
Basantpur Durbar (left).

Windows in the pedestal-building
of the Degutale temple, which
have typical horizontal
alignment.

The Jagannath temple, to the north of the Durbar Square, Kathmandu. The erotic scenes with small figures at the foot of the roof-struts illustrate—along with comparable statuary from the animal world— the Tantric sex practices. These carvings have their origins in the workshop of Laksminarasimha Malla, around 1633 A.D.

fled from the Muslim invaders entering India. The raid of Nepal by the Muslim troops in 1349 A.D. under Shams-ud-Din Ilyas produced few lasting effects. The period of the early Malla kings (from 1200 to 1482 A.D.) is considered to be the golden era of Nepalese culture. New towns were established, many palaces and temples were constructed and cultural exchanges took place between Tibet, India and Nepal. A new calendar was introduced: Buddhism was driven away by Hinduism.

The early Malla period came to an end with the death of King Jayayaksha in 1482 A.D. His sons split the stable and united kingdom into three independent kingdoms: Kathmandu, Patan and Bhaktapur. They fought with one another but they also acted as sources of inspiration for one another during the times of the late Malla kings (1482 to 1768 A.D.). Temples, palaces and pillars are eloquent witnesses of these times. The rule of the Shah dynasty (the Gurkhas) has formed the Kingdom's recent history. The dynasty, which continues to govern the country, seized power in the 18th century. A phase of military expansion ended with the repelling of the Nepalese troops by the British and the signing of the Peace Treaty with the East India Company. The royal family lost power substantially between 1848 and 1951: the Prime Ministers of the Rana family let the country slide into utter backwardness and isolation. With the bloodless revolution of 1951 and the coming to power of King Tribhuvan, Nepal took the plunge into the 20th century; under his grandson, King Birendra, the country has been trying to keep its balance.

Kathmandu, Indra Chowk: Akasha Bhairava temple. The window in the first floor offers the presiding deity a view of the goings-on in the market-place below. Prayer-flags, pillars and arches are gilded. The chopped-off head of a Kirati monarch is said to be inside the huge Bhairava mask.

Patan, Durbar Square: A row of temples marks the view of the palace. In the foreground is the temple of the youthful god, Krishna (Jayasim Deval, 1722 A.D.); behind it is the Taleju bell (1736 A.D.) and the Hari-Shankar temple (1705 A.D.). In the background is the Vishvanatha (1676 A.D.) and the Bhimsen temple (1680 A.D.). The red banner on the Jayasim Deval temple is an election placard.

16

Patan, stone head of Garuda in Swatha, north of the Durbar Square. Garuda, the mount of the god, is praying on his knees in front of the small Vishnu temple. He himself is highly venerated, as is evident from the offerings. The statue and the temple date from the year 1706 A.D.

Patan, Palace, Mul Chowk:
The statues of the goddesses, Shri
and Lakshmi, flank the seat of
Taleju. They are also venerated
as river goddesses, Ganga and
Yamuna. The hand-gesture of the
goddess is a Mudra.

Patan, Palace, Mul Chowk:
The bronze statue of Lakshmi
flanks the entrance to the seat of
the goddess. She is standing on a
tortoise. The apparel produces an
effect of transparency. An artistic
finish has been given to the
drapery.

Patan, entrance-wall of Kva Bahal monastery. The richly-gilded monastery is dedicated to Gautama Buddha.

A small stone-sculpture in the neighbourhood of Kumbhesvara temple, in the northern part of Patan, depicts god Vishnu. Exhibited with his attributes, the god is seen seated on his mount, Garuda.

The Many Many Ways of God

Patan, Durbar Square: A view of the Garuda statue from the Vishvanath temple. The white Shikhara temple houses Narasimha. In the background stands the Hari-Shankar temple, which is dedicated to a manifestation of Vishnu and Shiva.

In this country, which is remarkable for the interaction between various religions, the beliefs have blended into a bewildering admixture. Hinduism is the state religion. It won the day against Buddhism many centuries ago. Nothing is recorded in the history of Nepal which speaks of major religious differences or wars. Buddhism is practised in its Mahayana form. The special forms of Tantric Buddhism and of Lamaism have been enlivened by refugees from Tibet. The Chini Lama, the third ranking Lama after the Dalai lama and the Panchen Lama, resides in a house near Boudhanath—the biggest stupa in the world. The Muslim faith never attained any foothold in Nepal. As a result of the blending of diverse religious beliefs, many holy places, such as the stupa of Swayambhunath, are frequented by Buddhists as well as Hindus. Some gods are considered by both the religions to be different manifestations of the same god. Thus Buddha is highly venerated in Hinduism as an incarnation of Vishnu and, similarly, to the Buddhists Buddha is an incarnation of Vishnu.

The caste system, otherwise not customary in Buddhism, was prevalent here way back in the 14th century A.D., though never practised with the same vigour and severity as in India. To the Nepalese the gods are not abstract beings; they are real, existing together, as it were, with human beings. From this standpoint, the naturalness of the ceremonial, with which a religious rite is carried out, becomes easily explainable. When, in the course of an actual ritual, various objects are touched and God's grace descends on the human beings by the offerings of vermilion powder, saffron as well as various animals, these are seen as attributes of ordinary life. These daily Pujas in the smal-

Balaju: The statue of Jalasayanarayana in a rectangular tank which is symbolic of the primordial ocean. God Vishnu rests on the cosmic serpent and is meditating amidst his works of creation. Two more images of this type exist in the Kathmandu Valley; one in the King's Palace in Kathmandu (inaccessible), and the other in Buddha Nilakantha. All these sculptures date from ancient times.

ler temples in the neighbourhood, or in one's own house, are specially important. In course of time, some of the big temples lost their importance for the common folk and became merely places of tourist interest.

In times of yore, the primitive religions carried on without idols. The ceremonial was limited to a sacrificial rite on an altar without any iconical or non-iconical representation. There are many holy places in Nepal, where a stone, a spring or a tree is still considered to be an abode of God. The rep-

The Durbar Square of
Bhaktapur was originally
situatedd on the outskirts of the
town. Stone-lions guard the
entrance to Vatsala temple
(constructed in the Shikhara
style) and to the (Napalese,
double-storeyed) Yaksheshvar
temple. The two-storeyed Shiva-
temple is a replica of the
Pashupatinath temple. King
Bhupatindra Malla sits praying
in front of the Sundhoka (left).

Bhaktapur, Tajapala Tole.
Lotus pillar with cobra and
dragon in front of Bhimsen
temple.

Bhaktapur: Golden Gate and Palace of the 55 Windows.
The Golden Gate (Sundhoka) is the entrance to the palace area of the
Mul Chowk and to the abode of goddess Taleju Bhawani. In 1325
A.D. Prince Harasimhadeva was chased away from his Indian capital
by the Muslims. He came to the Kathmandu Valley. He had brought
along with him his house goddess Taleju Bhawani and, thanks to the
mysterious power of the goddess, the city-dwellers offered him the reign
of their city. He thereafter constructed the Mul Chowk. The gate of the
Sundhoka was set into both parts of the palace in the year 1753 A.D.
The portal-border is formed by symbols, portending luck, and statues of
gods. The palace was constructed by Bhupatindra Malla. The lower
storeys of the palace have windows of various sizes.

resentation of gods in the temples is mostly iconical. However, symbols, like the *lingam* of god Shiva,
are highly venerated. In the case of statues, the
body-and hand gestures, colour and physical attributes serve as signs of indentification. The Hindu
animal-mounts, standing on a pedestal in front of
the temples, indicate the deity, to whom the holy
place is dedicated. The Nandi bull is the mount of
Shiva, the mythological bird, Garuda, pertains to
Vishnu and the rat proclaims the presence of the
elephant-headed god, Ganesha.

Bhaktapur, Durbar Square, Siddhi-Lakshmi temple (also Durga temple)
Southern side with statues of guards.
Behind is the King's Palace (1695 A.D.)
The stone images of the guards correspond to the same increasing power principle as in the case of the considerably bigger Nyatapola temple.

Bhaktapur, Sundhoka: In the centre of the door-panel, above the entrance, stands the many-faced, multi-armed goddess Taleju Bhawani. The statue has quite an imposing presence, owing to its posture. Garuda and Naga flank the goddess who is seated on the lotus pedestal.

Patan, King's Palace: Window in a courtyard (right above) Bhaktapur, Taumadhi Tole.
Gilded window on the eastern side of the Bhairava temple. The wood-carvings are covered with gilded embossings. The canopy-crowned tympanum carries the ubiquitous Garuda-Naga-Makara motif.

Divine Service in Thousand Forms

Many festivals are celebrated during the course of the Nepalese year. The Newars, the people of the Kathmandu Valley, have the most pompous celebrations and processions. The roots of most of these festivals go back to Hinduism and Buddhism. The actual contents and purpose of the festivals along with the elaborate paraphernalia are determined by tradition. Festivals in big towns are extravagant processions where scenes are enacted very much according to the rules of stagecraft. Smaller festivals are often organized by certain groups.

The domestic celebrations constitute the base of all such festivals. These family occasions mark the various stages in the life of an individual. The first occasion for celebrations is the birth, for the soul gets a fresh chance to escape the cycle of re-birth and come closer to *Nirvana* during the new life. During the rice-feeding ceremony, the Nepalis celebrate not only the child's switching over to solid food but also an effort is made at the same time to predetermine the child's prospects for a profession and his or her future in general. Hindu boys don the holy thread at the age of thirteen while Buddhist boys of similar age get initiated into monastic life by moving from door to door. Young girls before puberty are married in the temple of the elephant-headed Ganesha to god Narayan (Vishnu). In this ceremony, the rites of the actual, later marriage ceremony are carried out in anticipation. Vermilion powder is sprinkled on the head, finger nails are polished red. In rural areas, the marriage partner is mostly selected by the parents. In towns, the young people mostly find their partner on their own. The official engagement ceremony, accompanied with speeches and presents, is followed by the actual marriage ceremony for

29

which the auspicious time is determined by the priest: this ceremony may last up to a week.

In a country with low life-expectancy, special honour is accorded to aged people. At the age of 77 years, 7 months and 7 days, the person celebrates his 'jubilee' by repeating the rice-eating ceremony of childhood. He is taken through the city, ceremonially, in a carriage by his offspring.

The death provides the last occasion for family rites. The dead person is carried on a bier to the nearest river. After certain rituals, a stack of wood is prepared and the corpse is laid on it. The eldest son, or, the nearest relative, sets the funeral pyre on fire. After the cremation, the relatives take a bath in the river, put on white clothes and immerse the ashes of the deceased person in the water. Those who can afford prefer an important cremation ground like that of the Pashupatinath temple, on the Bagmati river, in Kathmandu. In the mountainous areas of the Himalayas, where there is scarcity of water and fire-wood, the dead bodies are hung on trees to be eaten away by vultures.

Apart from these family rites, there are occasions which are noteworthy only for particular castes and for social associations. The important festivals of the main religions present a variegated picture. Some are observed periodically, such as the blood sacrifice for goddess Dakshinkali, when even the otherwise vegetarian Hindus are permitted to consume the sacrificed animals. Other festivals take place annually; often a temple is needed for a single day or a rite. The anniversary of the founding of the State, or the King's birthday, are other festival occasions. Thus the traveller can rest assured that he shall be able to witness one festival or the other during his stay in Nepal.

Bhaktapur, Taumadhi Tole:
View of the Bhairava temple
(around 1600 A.D., restored
1934 A.D.) from Nyatapola
temple. The pedestal-less temple
with a rectangular foundation is
dedicated to the terrific aspect of
Lord Shiva. As is the case with
all rectangular temples, the main
deity is housed in the first floor
(left). It is hidden behind the
five-part carved and gilded
wooden window (right). The
roof-props have the statues of the
Tantric Ashtamatrikas (eight
mother-goddesses).

Abodes of Gods

Bhaktapur, Tajapala Tole, Dattatreya temple: Dattatreys temple (1427 A.D.) rises above one of the oldest areas of Bhaktapur. The god Dattatreya has his origin in south India and is on a level with the Triad of Brahma, Vishnu and Shiva. That is why we find in front of the temple symbols for Vishnu (Garuda on the pillar) as well as for other gods. The wrestlers, Jaya Malla and Phatta Malla, guard the temple entrance.

Earthquakes, decay caused by climatic conditions and armed conflicts led to the destruction of many monuments in Nepal. The use of wood and air-dried bricks set limits to the durability of the structures. In spite of diligent restoration work, a continuous decay of artistically significant monuments has been noticed. In the Kathmandu Valley alone, there are more than 2000 religious shrines and about 300 comparatively larger pagodas have been identified. In Kathmandu there are 24 big temples and more than 120 monasteries.

The Nepalese temple differs substantially from its Indian counterpart in its choice of construction material and its shape. The typical form is a two five-roofed pagoda, standing on a pedestal with a ground plan. The tower-like upper part of the stupa could have influenced this particular form of construction. The temples with a square ground-plan stand mostly on a three- to five-steps base. The actual temple towers over it in the form of a brick structure having rich wood-decoration on the doors, roofs and supports. The lower storey of the central building houses the worship room with the main deity which is a statue or a symbol of the god venerated. The upper storeys, mostly accessible only through ladders, are not used for any religious ceremonies. Older structures resemble pigrim houses, where balcony-type passages with low railings provide additional space. The roof-framework, pillars and supporting beams of wood are the abode and statue of the gods. The supporting beams are richly carved and have a 40 to 60 degree angle of inclination. The doors and door-frames and the door-panels over them have statues of gods, embellished with ornamental borders. A bell-shaped *Gajura* with a brass umbrella crowns the temple roof. In front of many temples, the car-

Bhaktapur, Taumadhi Tole, Nyatapola temple: The five-storeyed pagoda-style Nyatapola temple is situated on the northern side of the palace on a pedestal having five steps. The deity in the sanctum sanctorum is hidden. Nyatapola means: with five roofs. The south side of the pedestal produces a specially prominent effect through the statues of the guards. The wrestlers, Jaya Malla and Phatta Malla, had reputedly ten times as much prowess as a normal human being. Each of the elephants, lions and griffins are ten times stronger, in the respective order. At the top of the statues guarding the temple are the Tantric goddesses, Singhini and Baghini.

Pashupatinath: It is said that once Lord Shiva and Parvati were living in the groves, on the ravines of the Bagmati river, in the form of gazelles. That is why Lord Shiva is worshipped as Pashupatinath—the Lord of the animals. The two-storeyed, main temple is one of the oldest surviving monuments in the country.

rier-animal is found kneeling over a pedestal: this reveals the identity of the god in the inner temple. The major trend in the case of some buildings constructed later is determined by the pairs of guards on the pedestal steps.

The Nepalese temple developed from the festival-and pilgrim-house, that has a thick-set look as in the case of the oldest existing temple of the 16th century A.D. The Shiva temple of Pashupatinath (in Kathmandu) is a two-tier pagoda structure with an emphasis on the horizontal effect. In course of time, the stress shifted to higher and vertical forms. The glorious examples of the temple construction work are the big monuments, the three-storeyed Taleju temple of Kathmandu, the 5-storeyed Nyatapola temple of Bhaktapur and the Kumbeshvara temple of Patan. The last-named temple appears somewhat less impressive due to the absence of pedestals.

Special forms of temples are the Bhairava temples, which have no pedestals but have the rectangular ground plan. The protection of the god and the might of the ruler were supposed to be manifested in a palace temple standing on a big pedestal structure, which towered high over the king's residence. In the urban areas, there are buildings whose ground floor is used for mundane activities. From the sanctum sanctorum in the upper storey, the diety watches over the deeds of the people.

The Shikhara temples which are easily distinguished had their origins in north India. Made of unplastered stone fragments or bricks, slender and pillar-like, these project into the sky in a sweeping line. The temples have no sanctum sanctorum but have niches with images of gods. These structures date from the Malla period.

*Dakshinkali: In a ravine, situated to the south of Kathmandu, animal sacrifice is offered to Dakshinkali—(*Dakshin = south*)—the 'Kali of the south'. The dripping blood of the sacrificed animals is sprinkled on the main idol of goddess Kali and statues of the other* Matrikas *(mother-goddesses). The sacrificial animals must be of uncastrated male species. It is said that the goddess herself gave a Malla king instructions to construct this shrine.*

Holy Places

Holy places of Buddhism consisted originally of square courtyards, of the dimensions of a Ropini (an old Nepalese square measure = 526 sq. m.). The Mul Chowks of Patan and Bhaktapur are examples of Hindu shrines of similar design. A stupa was often erected in the middle of Buddhist shrines, while in the middle of the Hindu courtyards stood a temple. The projecting courtyard roofs were supported by richly decorated props; the latter stood in iconographic coherence with the roof supports of the temple.

One finds important shrines in the suburbs of the cities; these are sprawled in all directions and are dedicated to different manifestations of the same god.

Monastic life, as understood in a Christian monastery, was unknown to the Buddhist wandering monks. During the rainy (monsoon) season, the latter sought shelter in the multi-shaped monasteries (*Viharas*). The Nepalese monastery matches the ornate residences of the Newari style. Brick structures with carved windows make up the square courtyards and around these are lined up dwelling units and monastic cells.

Pashupatinath, Ghats: Cremation ground below the Arya Ghat (left).

Pashupatinath, Arya Ghat: The flight of stairs leads to the Shiva temple on the bank of the sacred Bagmati river. The proximity of water is important for every Hindu shrine owing to continual ritual bathing. The water thus serves religious purposes, more so than the hygienic ones. The cremation spots for the royal family are located near the temple. The entry to the temple complex is barred to non-Hindus.

Pashupatinath: In the temple complex of goddess Rajarajeshwari, towards the south, stands the 11th century statue of Gautama Buddha. Though sunken in the ground, this statue exudes calm and peace. The Buddha statue in a Hindu shrine is indicative of the earlier hegemony of Buddhism.

Changu Narayan: Relief-sculpture of Narasimha (13th century A.D.) The man-lion Narasimha, an incarnation of god Vishnu, tears out the heart of the demon-king Hiranyakashipu. On the right stands Prahlada. Under his feet lies the crown which has fallen from the demon's head. To the left of Vishnu stand Lakshmi and the winged Garuda. Above the scene hover lords Shiva, Brahma and Indra. The Nagas (serpents) below are symbolic of the underworld, towards which one hand of the demon is pointing.

Banepa, Chandeshwari temple: Goddess Parvati, the consort of Lord Shiva, has been graphically represented on the side-wall of the temple as the slayer of demons.

Pokhara: A Sadhu near a Bindhyavasini temple.

Abodes of Human Beings

Nepalese towns convey the impression of their European counterparts in the Middle Ages. Multi-storeyed houses stand pressing against one another on scanty space. Narrow bypaths lead to small squares. The optimal utilisation of the available area has taken place. The sources of water are the focal point of public life. The craftsmen and traders carry on their business on the ground floor. The upper floors are used for residential purposes and directly, under the roof, through whose slits smoke comes out, we can locate the kitchen. In many places, as perhaps in Kirtipur, the only sign of the twentienth century is provided by the electric cables. The King's palace and the big temple-squares are the centres of town life. In olden days, big palaces and colonies are said to have existed at what are now solitary shrines like Changu Narayan. The direct link between the shrines of the gods and the ruler's residence in a complex legitimised the power of the kings as well as their divine right to rule. The invasion by Muslims (in 14th century A.D.) and the periodic occurrence of terrible earthquakes spared little that was old, The towns carry many marks of the building activities that took place during the Malla period. The rivalry amongst the city-kingdom led to the construction of opulent palaces and temples, each one supposed to glorify the builder.

The palaces of the Malla kings are multi-storeyed brick-structures, bedecked with carved, wooden windows, balustrades and column-supported bays. These buildings are spread over several courtyards. Some courtyards served as the abodes of gods. Small towers stand at the corners of these courtyards. The Mul Chowk, the seat of the household goddess Taleju, forms the centre of the palace. The ruler never used the square courtyard, with the prop-supported roof, for residential purposes; it was used only for religious ceremonies. The buildings of the Rana rulers bear the imprint of the architectures of the 19th century which was permeated with European influence. These buildings differ markedly from traditional Nepalese structures.

The Newari residence, on the other hand, is a secluded unit and is not very attractive. Inside, life in the joint family runs its set course around the small courtyard, where the family-god has his abode. He is there for the protection and welfare of the inmates. The worship (*puja*) of the family-god is a normal everyday chore of the householder.

Palaces as well as homes don't have any glass windows; instead there are window-lattices which are put together artistically. The first glass-pane in Nepal was a gift to King Bhupatendra Malla (1696–1722 A.D.), who had this costly item fixed in his palace with great pride. The first house with glass windows in Kathmandu was built in the middle of the 19th century.

Changu Narayan: Gilded bronze statue of King Bhupatendra Malla, the founder of the temple of Changu Narayan. On a journey to India his widow installed (1704 A.D.) the statues of the founder in a small shrine in front of the Western-style entrance to the temple.

Masterly Craftsmanship

The art of the wood-carver evolved to its full capacity under the Malla kings. The construction boom in the rival city-kingdoms during the late Malla period, the imitation craze of the rich nobility and an unlimited supply of raw materials, provided, cumulatively, the right incentives for the development of the art. The brick was the chosen construction-material for temples as well as residential buildings. The wooden windows having fantastic variations in carvings and dark-staining stood out markedly in these structures. The facade of Newari buildings was symmetrical. Other buildings had horizontally-oriented windows; the actual window-lattice was almost square-shaped. Later on, higher and vertically-oriented windows came into vogue. The window-lattices, assembled by different laths, assumed more and more playful and artistic forms. The window-frames consisted of two parts jutting into one another, bigger part on the inner side and the smaller part on the outer side. These frames were held together by wooden nails and by mortise and tenon. The horizontal frame parts stuck out of the actual window and thus the horizontal effect was pronounced.

The temple doors are choice spots for wood—carved reliefs. Images stand—watching the passage from the profane to the holy world-in the interior of the temple. On both sides of the doors stand goddesses riding on a *Makara*—a mythical figure, half dragon, half crocodile. The carved representations on the doors are not in the figure-form only; symbols or signs as harbingers of luck were used for decoration. In rich temples the wood-carvings were sometimes covered by copper or gilded bronze.

Kathmandu, Jagganath temple: Support with the statue of a multi-faced god on a lotus. Below is a couple engaged in erotic sex-play. Above: leaves of a tree (left)

Changu Narayan: The triple-door of Vishnu temple (on the west side) is crowned with a tympanum. The old temple was destroyed in a fire in 1702 A.D.. The existing structure was consecrated in the presence of the three rulers of the Kathmandu Valley in 1708 A.D. The sanctum sanctorum is open on all sides: the main deity, revered by Buddhists as a manifestation of Lokeshvara, however, remains hidden from view. The wood carving was replaced by gilded embossings.

Above the door leading to the sanctum sanctorum there is a semicircular frame; the portrayal on this tympanum is almost always similar. Garuda, the winged mount of Vishnu, is seen flying in the crown area. Garuda has several serpents (*nagas*)—his preys—in his mouth and in his fangs. The serpents make up the frame of the arch up to the lower end where two *Makaras* serve as the dead end. In the centre of the arch, there are figures of the presiding deity and his retinue. The obliquely protruding wooden struts of the temple-roofs are ideal places for adhoc artistic portrayal. It was here that the imagination of the Nepalese woodcarver could soar to great heights in the creation of figure-motifs. The slender figure-area is divided into three parts. The central, the largest area, depicts the god in human or animal form; several arms carry the attributes and signs of the god. Whether it was the Tantric mother-goddesses, the terrifying aspects of the gods, or the various manifestations of the god residing in the temple, all of these were depicted with great finesse. Many images lift a hand towards the upper arch which consists of a more or less outlined and symbolised foliage of a tree. Originally wood-nymphs were carved on props, a form of representation which is still in vogue. There are gnomes squatting on rugged rocks under the feet of the main statue. In some temples, erotic scenes portray man's effort to be very close to gods, and *Nirvana*, in the course of the Tantric love play.

Newars remain unsurpassed in Asia for their creations in wood. No other people achieved such a high degree of perfection in the execution of an immense and intricate variety of forms.

*Changu Narayan temple:
Representation of god Vishnu as
man-lion, tearing out the heart of
a demon. The hands carry the
symbols of the god; the discus,
conch, club, etc.*

*No limits can be set as regards
variations in the portrayal of the
gods.*

Bajrajogini, Sekh-Narayan temple: Not far from Parphing, at the foot of the Gorakhnath hill, a single-roof Narayan temple is pressed close to a rock face. Few tourists visit this temple. Prayer flags flutter in the wind. With every breeze, another prayer shall reach the gods.

Panauti, Brahmayani temple (1617 A.D.): This fully-restored temple (on the bank of the Bagmati) is dedicated to the chief goddess of a small Newari community in the Banepa valley. The three-roofed village temple is the starting-point of an annual chariot procession. Legends mention an ancient kingdom in Panauti during the pre-Licchavi period; recent excavations have supported this belief.

Banepa, Chandeshvari temple: Bronze tympanum (door panel), on the northern side. The fearful monster, Chanda, haunted the Banepa Valley, from whose clutches they were saved by goddess Parvati. The inhabitants erected a temple to Parvati (as Chandeshvari, the slayer of the demon) for having come to their aid. The central part of the frieze has been renovated.

Scene in Dakshinkali: Crowds of devotees who assemble here during the sacrificial celebrations attract beggars as well as street-vendors. The little girl waits patiently for her mother, who is begging for alms.

Swayambunath, Stupa: tympanum above the shrine Ratnasambhava on the southern side. The present form of the Buddha shrine goes back to the times of Pratap Malla. This explains the typically Hindu Garuda-Naga-Makara tympanum. The serpents have a special significance in Swayambunath— they bring rains to the Kathmandu Valley.

Understanding the gods

Normally, only stone-sculptures survived from the olden times. Steles from the classical period of the Licchavi era (5th to 8th century A.D.) are found mostly in Changu Narayan. In these sculptures (in stone), the harmony in the proportions, the delicacy of the contours and the artist's control over his material, are simply fascinating. The statues look slender, elegant and almost transparent and ethereal. During the post-classical period (9th to 13th century A.D.) there was preference for over-slender, stretched figures. Most of the sculptures in wood date from the baroque Malla era. The craftsmen were in the service of the rulers and the rich nobility.

Swayambunath: The shrine of Buddha Akshobhya, the eastern transcendental Buddha.

Swayanbunath, Sitala-Devi temple and votive stupas: The small temple stands on a plateau near the big stupa compound. It is venerated by the Hindus and the Buddhists alike. To Buddhists the goddess Hariti is the guardian deity for children; the Hindu goddess Sitala protects during the smallpox epidemic.

Swayambunath, Votive stupas; Sitala-Devi temple and stupa as viewed from the north-west: In the background (left in the picture) rises the Shikhara tower dating from the Malla times. The oldest inscription says that under King Manendra (5th century A.D.) a monastery was constructed at this place. Perhaps the exposed part of Swayambunath was used for cult purposes much earlier. The eyes of Harmika symbolise Bodhisattva Avalokiteshvara, who is worshipped in the Kathmandu Valley as Machhendranath. He watches everything, knows everything and, can, however, also forgive everything. (right)

The Eyes of Buddha

Boudhnath Stupa seen from the north-west: The stupa is situated on the ancient trade route connecting Kathmandu with Tibet. The base has such fine measurements that a 'reflection' of the hemisphere below would touch the ground. With its 40-metre diameter, Boudhnath is the biggest stupa in Nepal.

The stupa, the symbol of Buddha attaining *Nirvana*, is the most important and the most impressive architectural form in Buddhism. The cult object has great plasticity and is held to be the seat of Buddha Vairojana and the four transcendental Buddhas. The word 'stupa' originally meant 'hair-bun', 'summit' or 'mountain' (now it means: 'grave-monument'). In pre-Buddhist times it was customary in north India to erect burial-mounds near a road-crossing for princes and holy men; actually it was a custom prevalent in the whole of Eurasia.

When Gautama Buddha desired to be buried in this manner, this particular architectural form attained a special religious significance. There were wars between some states and principalities for the acquisition of the ashes of the founder of the religion. A Brahmin settled the dispute by giving one-eighth part of the ashes to each claimant. The first eight Buddhist stupas came into existence in this manner.

These monuments were opened up under Emperor Ashoka and the ashes were distributed among the thousand stupas erected by him. A difference is discernible among various stupas: some have mortal remains of the historical Buddha and other holy men; while some have no relics. In each case, however, there is faith in the all-pervading presence of the Enlightened One.

The ground-plan of a stupa shows a cosmic diagram: a *Mandala*. It is formed by the base lines of the pedestal, the hemispherical body, a low stone-chest over the *anda* (*anda* = egg) of quadratic layout (*harmika*) on which Buddha's eyes are painted; these eyes look out into the world and watch the affairs of mankind. Above this rise steps which are held by a pole anchored in the *anda*.

The view of the stupa from the south: A group of houses surrounds the complex. The Buddhist pantheon is represented in the 108 small niches circling the hemisphere at the ground level.

These symbolise the difficult path to *Nirvana*. The top is crowned with a three-fold umbrella. Five shrines around the hemispherical *anda*, or a row of many small niches, are arranged according to the directions of the compass and contain cult images of the transcendental Buddha. The stupa does not have any passage nor any grave chamber. Around the shrine there are fences or rows of prayer wheels. The worship (*Puja*) of Buddha consists in going round the shrine many times in the clockwise direction, thus symbolically completing the course of the sun. The place becomes the symbol for the central point of the earth as well as the symbol for Buddha.

Kirtipur: At the Holi festival, a priest puts a Mandala *round a small stupa, which reminds one of the four-faced Shiva* lingam. *Vermilion powder and flower garlands are regarded as some of the essential offerings.*

Chabahil, a small stupa with the shrines of the transcendental Buddhas and a stair-type pinnacle.
According to the legend, the daughter of Emperor Ashoka is said to have founded a monastery here. The stupa is situated on an important crossing on the ancient Indo-Tibet route. This stupa has no pedestal and is one of the oldest shrines in the Kathmandu Valley.

Bajrajogini: Surrounded by pictures of gods, a Guru sits, meditating, near the Sekh Narayan temple.

Girls and women carry loads, supported by head-bands. The nose-ring reveals the identity of the tribe to which one belongs (right).

Terrace landscape with Newar houses in Dhulikhel, in the eastern mountains, around Kathmandu (right below)

Himalaya: View of Makalu (8475 m.) from south-west.

Pokhara: View of the western Himalaya giants from the Phewa lake. Extreme left: Dhaulagiri (8167 m.); in the centre is the Annapurna massif with Machapucchare (6994 m.) and the Annapurna peaks; on the right is the Lamjung Himal (6986 m.) (right above).

Stupas are scattered on the ancient routes. (right below)

Thyangboche Monastery: Mani Rimdu festival of the Sherpas. Old 'demons' appear during some rituals; these are carried in processions once in four years. The traditional masks are decorated with much love and creative intelligence in ever new ways.